MIND TRICKS and

✷ ILLUSIONS ✷

to

BOGGLE
THE BRAIN

Jessica Rusick

Super Sandcastle

An Imprint of Abdo Publishing
abdobooks.com

abdobooks.com

Published by Abdo Publishing, a division of ABDO, PO Box 398166, Minneapolis, Minnesota 55439. Copyright © 2020 by Abdo Consulting Group, Inc. International copyrights reserved in all countries. No part of this book may be reproduced in any form without written permission from the publisher. Super SandCastle™ is a trademark and logo of Abdo Publishing.

Printed in the United States of America, North Mankato, Minnesota
102019
012020

 THIS BOOK CONTAINS RECYCLED MATERIALS

Design: Aruna Rangarajan, Mighty Media, Inc.
Production: Mighty Media, Inc.
Editor: Rachael Thomas
Design Elements: Shutterstock Images
Cover Photographs: Mighty Media, Inc., Shutterstock Images
Interior Photographs: Keystone/Stringer/Getty Images, p. 15; kravcs/iStockphoto, p. 8 (calculator); Mighty Media, Inc., pp. 7, 8, 9, 10, 11, 12, 13, 14, 16, 17, 18, 19, 20, 21, 23, 24, 25, 26, 27, 28, 29, 30, 31; Shutterstock Images, pp. 5, 6, 8 (cork), 9 (envelope), 18 (hands), 21 (kid), 22, 30 (group of kids); Wikimedia Commons, pp. 4
The following manufacturers/names appearing in this book are trademarks: Crayola®

Library of Congress Control Number: 2019943377

Publisher's Cataloging-in-Publication Data

Names: Rusick, Jessica, author.
Title: Mind tricks and illusions to boggle the brain / by Jessica Rusick
Description: Minneapolis, Minnesota : Abdo Publishing, 2020 | Series: Super simple magic and illusions
Identifiers: ISBN 9781532191596 (lib. bdg.) | ISBN 9781532178320 (ebook)
Subjects: LCSH: Magic tricks--Juvenile literature. | Sleight of hand--Juvenile literature. | Optical illusions--Juvenile literature. | Science and magic--Juvenile literature.
Classification: DDC 793.8--dc23

Super SandCastle™ books are created by a team of professional educators, reading specialists, and content developers around five essential components—phonemic awareness, phonics, vocabulary, text comprehension, and fluency—to assist young readers as they develop reading skills and strategies and increase their general knowledge. All books are written, reviewed, and leveled for guided reading and early reading intervention programs for use in shared, guided, and independent reading and writing activities to support a balanced approach to literacy instruction.

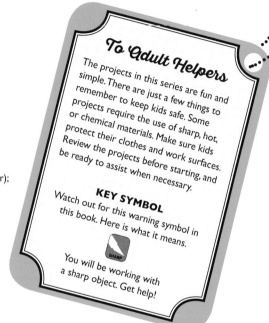

To Adult Helpers

The projects in this series are fun and simple. There are just a few things to remember to keep kids safe. Some projects require the use of sharp, hot, or chemical materials. Make sure kids protect their clothes and work surfaces. Review the projects before starting, and be ready to assist when necessary.

KEY SYMBOL

Watch out for this warning symbol in this book. Here is what it means.

SHARP
You will be working with a sharp object. Get help!

Contents

THE MAGIC OF
Mind Tricks and Illusions

Has someone ever read your mind? Or made an object spin with the power of thought? These are mind tricks and **illusions**!

Performers who practice this type of magic are called **mentalists**. Mentalists appear to read people's minds, see the future, and make objects move without touching them. But like all magic tricks, there are **techniques** and science behind each illusion.

Several mentalism acts have involved husband and wife teams.

Tips and Techniques

Mind tricks and **illusions** take preparation to pull off. Some use a method called forcing. This means controlling the choice a **volunteer** makes.

There are many ways to do this, but the result is always the same. The volunteer thinks they are choosing a **random** card, coin, or word. However, the magician already knows which choice the volunteer will make.

It is important to play up the **illusion** of choice when forcing a person's decision. Keep saying a trick is **random**, even though it's not. Get your **audience** to agree that there's no way you can **predict** the future or read someone's mind. That way, they will be even more shocked when you do!

1. Read the steps carefully.

2. Practice in front of a friend to figure out the best angle for a trick.

3. Come up with jokes and stories to **distract** your audience.

Remember, the brain is smart! Tricking it takes **precision**.

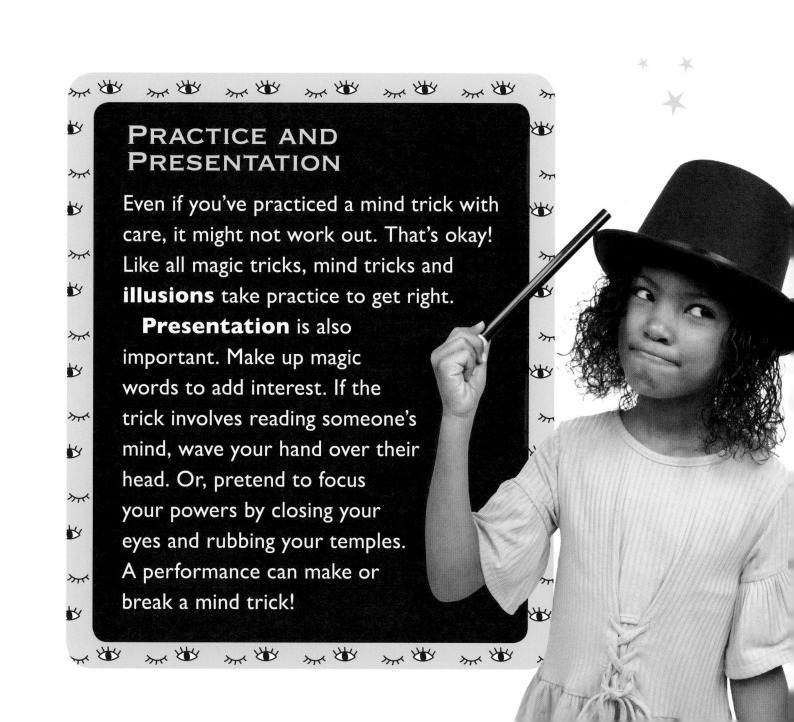

PRACTICE AND PRESENTATION

Even if you've practiced a mind trick with care, it might not work out. That's okay! Like all magic tricks, mind tricks and **illusions** take practice to get right.

   Presentation is also important. Make up magic words to add interest. If the trick involves reading someone's mind, wave your hand over their head. Or, pretend to focus your powers by closing your eyes and rubbing your temples. A performance can make or break a mind trick!

MENTALIST
Tool Kit

Here are some of the materials that you will need for the tricks in this book.

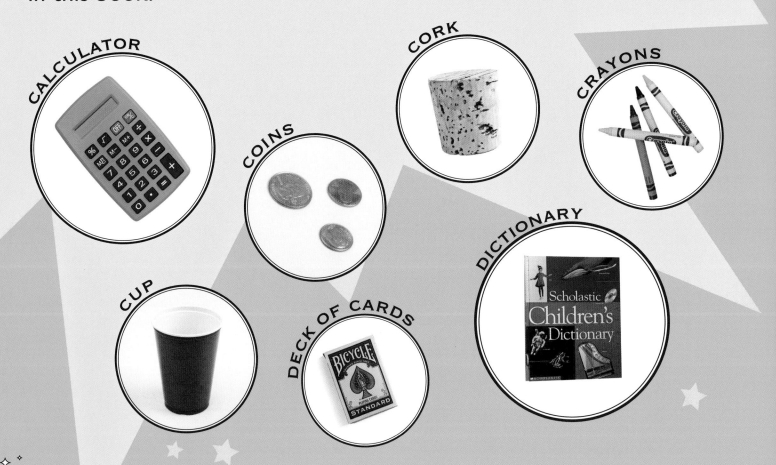

CALCULATOR

CORK

CRAYONS

COINS

CUP

DECK OF CARDS

DICTIONARY

ENVELOPE

MARKERS

INDEX CARDS

RULER

PENS

SCISSORS

PENCIL

NEEDLE

9

CRAYON PSYCHIC

Guess the right color every time!

1 Turn away from a **volunteer** with your hands behind your back. Ask the volunteer to put one of the crayons in your hands.

2 Tell your volunteer to hide the other crayons. Then, turn to face the volunteer.

3 Remind the volunteer that they could have chosen any crayon. While you talk, gently scrape the crayon wax with a fingernail. This will **transfer** a bit of color to your nail.

4 Ask the volunteer to think of the color they chose. Place your hand on their forehead, as if you are reading their mind. As you do, sneak a quick look at the color on your nail.

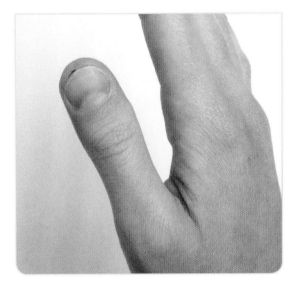

5 Pretend to read the volunteer's mind a bit longer. Then, tell them the color you scraped from the crayon. You're a mind reader!

MATH MAGIC

Guess a random word in the dictionary!

1 To prepare the trick, turn to page 108 of the dictionary. Count down to the ninth word on the page. Write the word on the piece of paper and place it in the envelope.

2 Ask a **volunteer** to name three different numbers between one and nine. Write the numbers in the notebook to form one three-digit number.

3 Ask the volunteer to **reverse** the number. Write this number in the notebook.

4 Have the volunteer subtract the lower number from the higher number. Write down the answer in the notebook.

CONTINUED ON NEXT PAGE

5 Have your **volunteer reverse** the answer from step 4. Write this number below the answer from step 4. If the answer from step 4 was 99, add a zero in front of the 99 before having your volunteer reverse it. So, instead of 99 and 99, it will be 099 and 990.

6 Tell your volunteer to add the two numbers from step 5 together. The answer will always be 1089. Write this number in the notebook.

7 Ask your volunteer to turn to page 108 of the dictionary you looked in earlier. Make sure you cannot see the page.

8 Have your volunteer count down to the ninth word on the page. Say that you saw this moment before it happened and already wrote down the word they are looking at. Then ask your volunteer to open the envelope and read that same word!

ICONIC ILLUSIONISTS

Sydney and Lesley Piddington were a husband and wife **mentalist** team in the 1940s. In one trick, Sydney asked **audience** members to put some writing or a drawing into envelopes. Later, he called Lesley, who  was somewhere miles away, and opened one envelope at **random**. Lesley read Sydney's mind and told him what was written down! To this day, there are many **theories** about the Piddingtons and their tricks.

YOU PICK, I PICK

Predict which object will be left over!

Scissors

Materials

+ an even number of random objects
+ piece of paper
+ pen
+ envelope

1 To prepare the trick, choose a small **random** object in the room without your **audience** knowing. This will be your secret object.

2 Write the name of your secret object on the piece of paper. Place it in an envelope and set it aside in the area where you will perform the trick.

3 Ask a **volunteer** to help you gather eight random objects from the room. Make sure your secret object is one of those chosen.

4 Ask your volunteer to point to any two objects. Remove one of the objects they choose. If one of the objects chosen is the secret object, remove the other object.

5 Now it's your turn. Point to any two objects that aren't the secret object. Have your volunteer remove one of the two objects.

6 Repeat steps 4 and 5 until only the secret object is left.

7 Tell your volunteer that you always knew which object would be left. Open the envelope and show them your **prediction**.

THREE-COLOR TELEPATHY

Make a surprise prediction!

Materials

+ 4 index cards

+ markers in 3 colors (blue, red, and yellow)

+ pen

+ envelope

+ pencil

1 Color one side of an index card red. Color one side of another card blue. Color one side of a third card yellow.

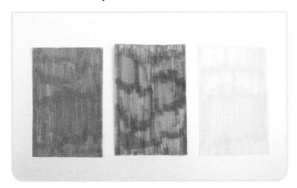

2 On the back of the blue card, write "You will choose blue" in pen.

3 On a fourth index card, write "You will choose yellow" in pen.

4 Place all four cards in an envelope with the colored cards in front.

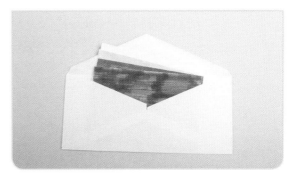

CONTINUED ON NEXT PAGE

5 Have an adult use the scissors to scrape off a small strip of paint on one side of the pencil.

6 Write "You will choose red" in pen on the pencil.

7 Set the pencil on the table where you will do the trick. Make sure the writing is not visible.

8 Now it is time to perform the trick. Remove the three colored cards from the envelope. Place them colored side up in front of your **volunteer**. Place the envelope near the pencil.

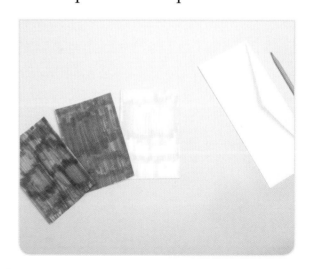

9 Tell the **volunteer** that you can see the future and know which of the three cards they will pick. Ask them to point to one of the colored cards.

10 If they choose the blue card, flip over the blue card to show your **prediction**.

11 If they choose the yellow card, ask your volunteer to open the envelope. Inside will be your prediction.

12 If they choose the red card, ask your volunteer to look at the pencil closely. They will see your prediction.

Cool

MIND-READING MASTER

Predict three random choices!

Materials

+ 1 non-clear cup

+ 3 different coins, one of which is a quarter

+ several colored markers or crayons

+ pen

+ 3 small pieces of paper

1 Place the cup, coins, markers, paper, and pen on a table.

2 Point to the markers. Tell your **volunteer** that you can see the future and know which color they will choose. Tell them you will write this color on a piece of paper.

3 On the paper, write, "quarter." Make sure no one can see what you are writing.

4 Fold the paper and place it in the cup.

5 Ask your volunteer to choose a marker. Set the other markers aside so you can remember which one they chose.

6 Say that you will now **predict** how many fingers the volunteer will hold up. On the second piece of paper, write the color of the marker the volunteer chose.

CONTINUED ON NEXT PAGE

7 Fold the second paper and place it in the cup.

8 Have the **volunteer** hold up however many fingers they would like. Remember the number they hold up.

9 Now tell your volunteer that you will **predict** which coin they will choose. On the third piece of paper, write the number of fingers the volunteer held up.

10 Fold the third paper and place it in the cup.

11 Place three coins in front of your volunteer and ask them to pick two. No matter which coins they pick, you want the quarter to be left over. This is called a force.

12 If the volunteer picks the two coins that aren't the quarter, remove them from the table and go to step 14.

13 If the **volunteer** picks the quarter and another coin, remove the third coin from the table. Have your volunteer pick again between the remaining two coins. No matter which coin they pick, remove the coin that is not the quarter.

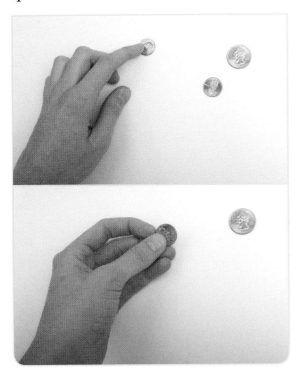

14 Remove the three pieces of paper from the cup. Carefully organize the "**predictions**" in order: marker color, number of fingers, and coin. One by one, reveal them to your volunteer.

PROP SWAP

As long as you force the volunteer's last choice, you can ask them whatever other questions you want. Try "predicting" their favorite ice cream flavor or movie. Or ask them to name a number between 1 and 1,000!

SNEAKY SHUFFLE

You'll always know which card they chose!

Materials
+ deck of cards

1 **Memorize** the bottom card in the deck.

2 Find a **volunteer**. Tell them you will shuffle the cards until they say "stop."

3 Hold the deck face down in your left hand. Move cards from the top of the pile over to your right hand. Keep all cards face down. Continue to move the cards from the top of the left pile to the top of the right pile until your volunteer says "stop."

4 Without looking at it yourself, show the bottom card in your left hand to the volunteer. Tell them to remember it. This is the card you memorized earlier.

5 Shuffle the whole deck of cards together. Tell the volunteer that you can find their card by reading their mind.

6 Pretend to read your volunteer's mind. Close your eyes and rub your temples. Then, pull out the memorized card from the deck!

PAPER TELEKINESIS

Make paper spin with your mind!

Materials

+ paper
+ ruler
+ scissors
+ cork
+ needle

1 Cut out a paper square that is 4 inches (10 cm) on each side.

2 Fold the square in half **diagonally**, making a triangle. Unfold the paper.

3 Fold the paper diagonally in the other direction. Unfold the paper.

4 Have an adult push the dull end of the needle into the center of the cork. About three-fourths of the needle should still stick out.

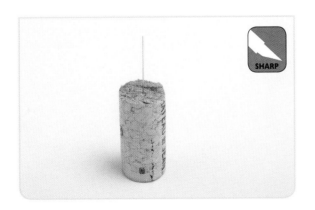

SHARP

5 Balance the paper square on the sharp end of the needle.

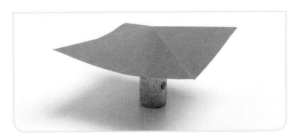

6 Cup your hands around the paper without touching it. The paper should spin! If it doesn't, warm your hands and try again.

BEHIND THE MAGIC

When you cup your hands around the paper, the warm air between your hands rises. Cool air then fills the space. This creates a **convection** current. The current causes the paper to spin!

HOST A MAGIC SHOW!

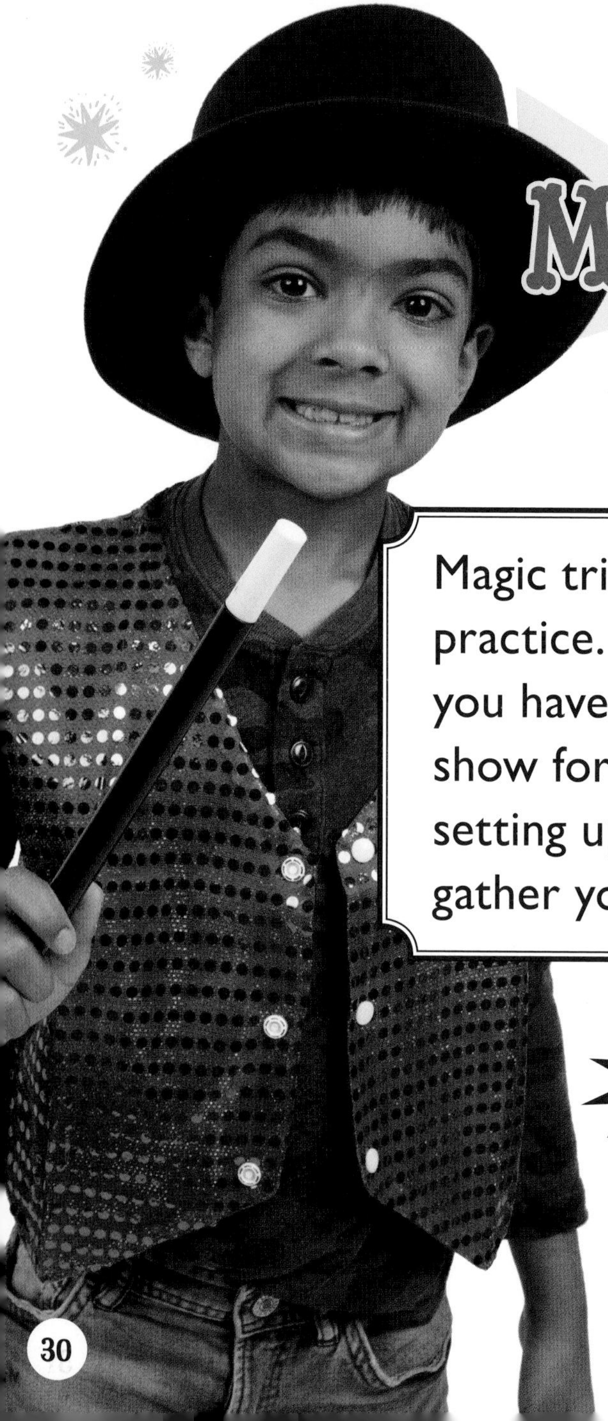

Magic tricks need more than **props** and practice. They also require an **audience**! When you have a few **illusions** ready, put on a magic show for your friends and family. You could try setting up a stage for it. Or, keep it simple and gather your audience around a table.

Whoa

Cool

TIPS TO BECOME A
Master Illusionist

Be **confident** when **presenting** your **illusions**.

Use stories and other **distractions** to make your performances stand out.

Keep an illusion's secret to yourself if you wish.
A little mystery makes magic fun!

Glossary of Magic Words

audience – a group of people watching a performance.

confident – sure of oneself.

convection – the movement of a gas or liquid in which the warm parts move up and the cool parts move down.

diagonal – at an angle.

distract – to cause to turn away from one's original focus of interest.

illusion – something that looks real but is not.

memorize – to learn by heart.

mentalist – a magician who performs mind tricks, such as mind reading.

precision – the quality or state of being accurate or exact.

predict – to say what will happen in the future. Something that is predicted is called a prediction.

present – to show or talk about something to a group or the public. A performance is called a presentation.

prop – an object that is carried or used by a performer in a performance.

random – without any order, purpose, or method.

reverse – backwards, in the opposite direction.

technique – a method or style in which something is done.

theory – an idea that explains how or why something happens.

transfer – to pass from one thing or place to another.

volunteer – a person who offers to do something.